READING ABOUT

Sounds

By Jim Pipe

Aladdin/Watts
London • Sydney

Quiet

Kevin and Jill are waiting for the parade. What sounds can they hear?

They hear the wind in the trees and a bird singing. It is quiet.

A mouse is very quiet.

Can you be as quiet as a mouse?

Loud

Bang! Bang! Bang!
What is that sound?

It is a hammer. It makes a loud sound. BANG! The bird flies away.

Brrm! Brrm! What is that sound?

It is a motorbike.

Far away, it sounds quiet.

Close up, it sounds very loud.

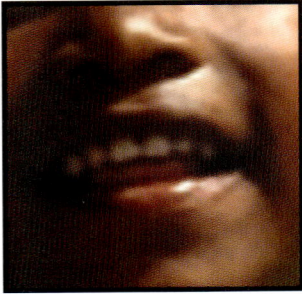

Talking

What is that sound?

It is Kevin talking. But Jill
wants to listen for the parade.
She puts a finger to her lips. Shh!

When you talk, you make sounds into words. When you read, letters stand for sounds.

Time sounds

Ding! Dong!

What is that sound?

It is the bell ringing.

It is 11 o'clock.

Time for the parade!

Some sounds make you jump.
An alarm clock says "Wake up".
The siren on a fire engine says
"Watch out"!

Machine sounds

Brrm! Brrm!

What is that sound?

Here come the trucks in the parade. Their engines rumble.

Some machines are noisy.

Others hum quietly.

This machine digs up the road.
It is very noisy. Cover your ears!

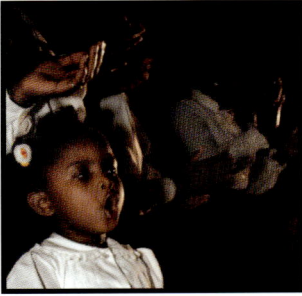

Voices

La-la-la! What is that sound?

That woman is singing!
The crowd shouts
and cheers.

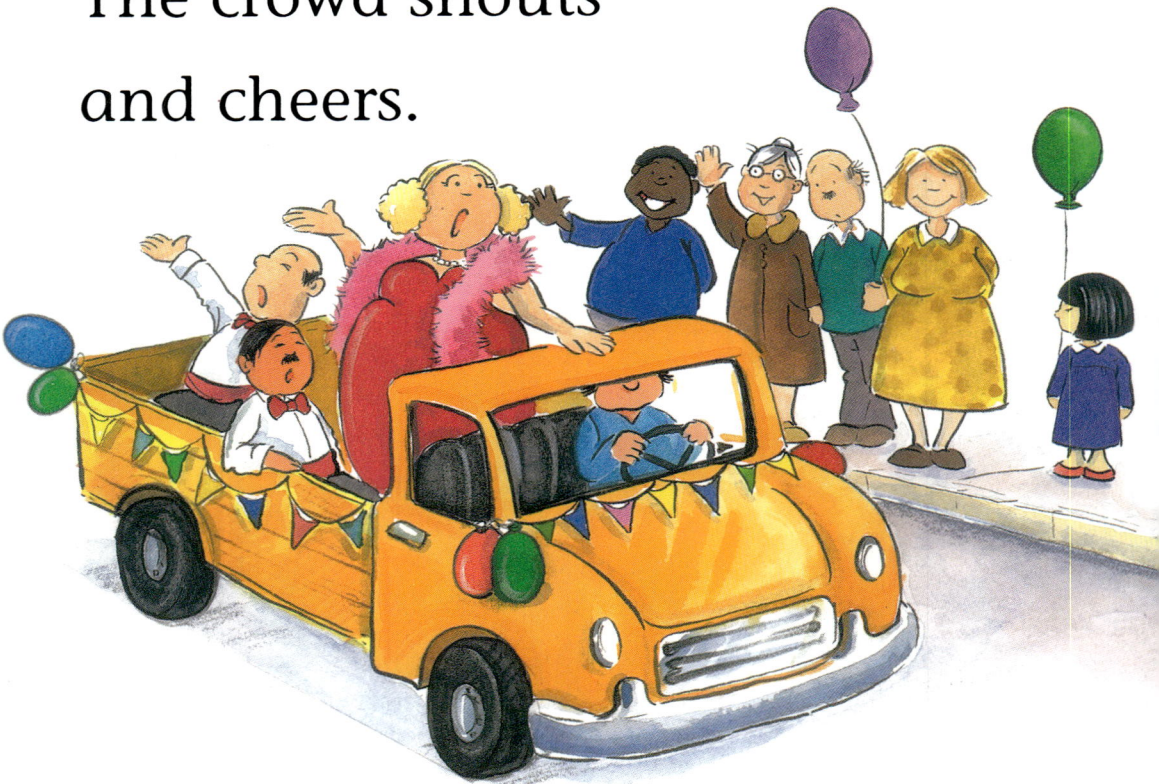

Your voice can make many sounds,
loud or soft, high or low.

What sounds can you make?
Can you hum, giggle and scream?

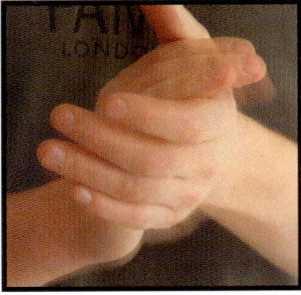

One, two, three, four

Tramp! Tramp! Tramp! Tramp!

What is that sound?

The parade is marching by.

The crowd claps.

14

Can you clap with your hands?
Clap! Clap! Clap! Clap!

This bird makes a sound with its
beak. Tap! Tap! Tap! Tap!

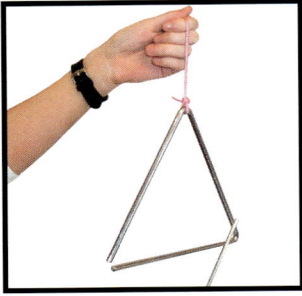

High and low

Boom! Boom! What is that sound?

It is a big drum.
It makes a
low sound.

A triangle goes
ding, ding!
It makes a
high sound.

ROAR! A bear makes a low sound.

You can hear it far away.

Can you roar like a bear?

Music

Da, da, da-da!

What is that sound?

The band is playing music.

The trumpets are very loud!

Music can make you feel happy.

It can make you dance!

It can make you sing!

Lots of noises

What is that sound?

The fireworks are going off.

Fireworks make a lot of noise.

Some fireworks whistle.

Some go whoosh!

And some just go BANG!

Here are some words about sound.

Quiet

Loud

High

Noisy

Low

These things make a sound.

Voice

Hammer

Hands

Band

Can you write
a story with
these words?

Bird

Do you know?

You can write down many sounds.

A clock goes
tick tock.

A cock goes
cock-a-doodle-doo!

Water goes
splash!

What sound does
a fire engine make?